*In My Own Words*

# The Diary of
# Elizabeth Bacon Custer,
## On the Plains with General Custer

Edited by Nancy Plain
Illustrations and map by Laszlo Kubinyi

BENCHMARK BOOKS

MARSHALL CAVENDISH
NEW YORK

Benchmark Books
Marshall Cavendish
99 White Plains Road
Tarrytown, New York 10591-9001
www.marshallcavendish.com

Library of Congress Cataloging-in-Publication Data

Custer, Elizabeth Bacon, 1842–1933.
[Diary. Selections]
The diary of Elizabeth Bacon Custer : on the plains with General Custer / edited by Nancy Plain ; illustrations and map by Laszlo Kubinyi.
p. cm. — (In my own words)
Summary: Presents the diary of the wife of General George Armstrong Custer, focusing on their life on the Great Plains from 1873 to 1876, when Custer and his Seventh Cavalry were clearing the way for the Northern Pacific Railroad and battling Native Americans. Includes bibliographical references and index.
1. Custer, Elizabeth Bacon, 1842–1933—Diaries—Juvenile literature. 2. Great Plains Description and travel—Juvenile literature. 3. West (U.S.)—Description and travel—Juvenile literature. 4. Custer, George Armstrong, 1839–1876—Juvenile literature. 5. United States. Army—Military life—History—19th century—Juvenile literature. 6. United States. Army. Cavalry, 7th—Juvenile literature. 7. Indians of North America—Wars—1866–1895 —Juvenile literature. 8. Army spouses—West (U.S.)—Diaries—Juvenile literature. 9. West (U.S.)—Biography—Juvenile literature. [1. Custer, Elizabeth Bacon, 1842–1933. 2. Army spouses. 3. Great Plains—Description and travel. 4. West (U.S.)—Description and travel. 5. Custer, George Armstrong, 1839–1876. 6. United States. Army—Military life—History —19th century. 7. United States. Army. Cavalry, 7th. 8. Indians of North America—Wars —1866–1895. 9. Women—Biography. 10. Diaries.] I. Plain, Nancy. II. Kubinyi, Laszlo, 1937– ill. III. Title. IV. Series: In my own words (Benchmark Books (Firm))

F594.C947 2004
973.8'2'092—dc21

2003001432

ISBN 0-7614-1647-1

Series design by Adam Mietlowski

Printed in China

1 3 5 6 4 2

*To Joyce Stanton, my editor, with thanks for her wisdom and encouragement*

# "BOOTS AND SADDLES"

## OR LIFE IN DAKOTA WITH GENERAL CUSTER

BY

ELIZABETH B. CUSTER

WITH PORTRAIT AND MAP

NEW YORK

HARPER & BROTHERS, FRANKLIN SQUARE

1885

*The title page of Elizabeth's book, "Boots and Saddles," from which this diary is taken*

# Elizabeth's Book

# *Introduction*

Elizabeth Bacon fell in love with George Armstrong Custer in 1862, when she was twenty years old. "Libbie," as she was called, had just graduated from a seminary for young women in her hometown of Monroe, Michigan. Custer, not yet twenty-three and only a year out of West Point, was already becoming famous as a Union cavalry commander, leading brilliantly successful — and daredevil — charges against the South in the Civil War. But because he was not from a socially prominent family, Libbie's father, a judge, disapproved of him. No matter. The young couple wrote letters in secret and met when Custer was able to visit Monroe on leave. In 1863 he played a decisive role in winning the Battle of Gettysburg for the North. That same year, too, he became the youngest man in the history of the army to be promoted to the rank of brigadier general. Now he was truly a national hero. Perhaps this softened the judge's attitude, because Libbie and "Autie," as Custer's family had nicknamed him, were married in 1864.

They must have been a striking couple to look at. Libbie had deep brown eyes and wavy brown hair; a "dark loveliness," one newspaper reporter would call her. And Autie was popularly known as the "Boy General with his flowing yellow curls." His cavalry uniform was

*Libbie as a young wife—"a dark loveliness,"
one reporter called her.*

*Autie at twenty-five—his Civil War exploits
earned him the nickname the "Boy General."*

colorful, too—a blue velveteen jacket, a red necktie, a general's gold star pinned to a floppy black hat. The Custers' honeymoon was interrupted when Autie was called back to fight in Virginia, but Libbie waited for him at nearby army headquarters. For the duration of the war, she followed him as closely as she could, and when that was not possible, she stayed in Washington, D.C. There she was introduced to President Abraham Lincoln, who shook her hand and said, "So this is the young woman whose husband goes into a charge with a whoop and a shout."

"Custer's Luck," they called it. The young general finished his Civil War career in spectacular fashion by cornering General Robert E. Lee's army at Appomattox, Virginia, thus helping to bring about the Confederate surrender, on April 9, 1865. Custer himself received the white flag of truce.

After the war, his shining reputation brought him tempting career offers in business and politics, but Custer was not made for office work. He loved military life too much to leave it. So in 1866, after spending a year with the army in Texas, the Custers traveled to Kansas so that Autie could assume command of the Seventh Cavalry. It had been created that year with the sole purpose of fighting the Indians of the Great Plains.

The Great Plains—that immense sweep of prairie that stretches westward from the Missouri River and rolls on all the way to the Rocky Mountains—had been home for centuries to many thousands of Native Americans. But to white Americans in the early 1800s, most of whom lived near the country's two coasts, the region seemed about as uninviting as the dark side of the moon. They called it the Great American Desert. As the century wore on, though, fur trappers and traders, miners, explorers, and pioneers saw that the Great Plains were not a desert at all. If these early travelers endured harsh weather and never-ending wind, they also found rich grasslands and abundant wildlife: ducks and turkeys feeding in the river valleys, deer and antelope grazing in the foothills, and buffalo everywhere—countless millions of the great, shaggy beasts.

Then in 1848, gold was discovered in California. Hordes of people bound for the Pacific coast began to cross the plains on the Oregon Trail. Some of them changed their minds halfway and stayed on the prairie to farm. Most of them did not see it this way, but they were trespassing on Indian land. And they were rapidly destroying the buffalo herds, upon which the Indians depended for almost every necessity of life.

During the Civil War, there was a lull in this white invasion. But after 1865, the United States government turned its attention once again to fulfilling the nation's "Manifest Destiny," to extending its control over the entire land, from sea to sea. This could not be accomplished safely, the government believed, until all the Plains tribes were confined to reservations. It would be better if they went peacefully, policy makers agreed, but if not, the army must force them. George Armstrong Custer was only one of several distinguished Civil War generals who were sent to do the job.

For most of the years between 1867 and 1876, the "Boy General" patrolled the wide prairie. And Libbie, who described herself as the "only officer's wife who always followed the regiment," went with him, moving from one army fort to another throughout the West. At first Custer was stationed in the southern plains. It was during his five-year stay in Kansas, from 1866 to 1871, that he established his reputation as an Indian fighter, particularly for a dawn attack on a Cheyenne village near the Washita River, in what is now the state of Oklahoma. If some Americans, mostly Easterners, called it an appalling massacre, others, mainly Westerners, were grateful to Custer for helping to stop Indian raids on their wagon trains, ranches, and settlements. But the real key to taming the region was in protecting from attack the men who were building the Kansas Pacific and Union Pacific railroads. Custer accomplished this, too. He pursued the tribes relentlessly, until by 1869 the majority of the Indians on the southern plains — southern Cheyennes, Kiowas, Comanches, Arapahoes — were living on reservations.

Indian fighting temporarily at a standstill, the Custers were sent by the army to Kentucky, where they lived from 1871 to 1873. Then General Philip Sheridan, commander of all army troops on the Great Plains, ordered Custer north to clear the way for the Northern Pacific Railroad. So Libbie and Autie embarked on a long, dangerous trip up the Missouri River with the Seventh Cavalry. Members of Custer's family also made the voyage: Autie's brother Colonel Tom Custer and his sister Margaret, who was married to the Seventh's Lieutenant James Calhoun. In April the travelers arrived at Fort Rice, in Dakota Territory. They moved once again, in the fall, to the newly built Fort Abraham Lincoln, on the shores of the Missouri. Although the fort was near the small town of Bismarck, the cavalry was truly in the wilderness. North and South Dakota, Wyoming, and Montana were not yet states then, just vast, windswept territories.

Even in this unfamiliar terrain, Custer was brimming with his usual confidence. "I could whip all the Indians on the continent with the Seventh Cavalry," he liked to say. But he did not reckon on the determination of the inhabitants of the Powder River Country, that remote region extending from the Black Hills, in present-day South Dakota, to the Bighorn Mountains, in Wyoming. There on the northern plains, bands of northern Cheyenne and Sioux clung passionately to the old ways, following the last large buffalo herd in the West. Warriors from these tribes, under the inspired leadership of Crazy Horse and Sitting Bull, were prepared to defend to the last ounce of their strength their right to live free. On June 25, 1876, these Cheyenne and Sioux clashed with the Seventh Cavalry at the Battle of the Little Bighorn. Custer and more than two hundred of his men were killed.

Before her wedding, Libbie had told Autie, "I had rather live in a tent with you than in a palace with another." And she meant it. Theirs was an intensely close marriage, although they had only twelve years together before Custer died in his disastrous "Last Stand." For the remaining fifty-seven years of her life — she died in 1933, almost ninety-one years old — Libbie devoted herself to honoring her husband's memory and defending his reputation against all attacks. In every way, he was her hero. She never questioned the role he had played in fighting the Plains Indians. She never questioned anything about him at all.

Elizabeth Custer channeled her loneliness after Custer's death into a writing career that supported her well. She wrote three accounts of her travels with "the general," as she respectfully refers to him in her books. The pages you are about to read are taken from Libbie's beautifully written *"Boots and Saddles"* or *Life in Dakota with General Custer*, published in 1885. (Its title refers to the bugle call "Boots and Saddles," which signals the cavalryman to mount his horse.) This work is a fascinating tale of army life on the northern plains when the West was still wild. It is also a love story, one woman's recollections of a time when she was young and happy. Looking back on those days, Libbie once wrote, "Blessed be our memory, which preserves to us the joys as well as the sadness of life!"

— Nancy Plain
Short Hills, New Jersey

*Dear Reader,*

*One of my motives in recalling these simple annals has been to give a glimpse to civilians of garrison and camp life. The isolation of the cavalry posts makes them quite inaccessible to travelers, and the risk of meeting warlike Indians does not tempt the visits of friends or even of the venturesome tourist. Our life, therefore, was often as separate from the rest of the world as if we had been living on an island in the ocean.*

*—Elizabeth Bacon Custer*
*1885*

# From Kentucky to Dakota: A Trip into the Unknown

[*March 1873*]

When orders came for the 7th Cavalry to go into the field again, General Custer was delighted. In Kentucky it had seemed an unsoldierly life, for a true cavalryman feels that a life in the saddle on the free open plain is his legitimate existence.

As soon as the officer announcing the order to move had disappeared, all sorts of wild hilarity began. From the first days of our marriage, General Custer celebrated every order to move with wild demonstrations of joy. His exuberance of spirits always found expression in some boyish pranks before he could set to work seriously to prepare for duty. I had learned to take up a safe position on top of the table; that is, if I had not already been forcibly placed there as a spectator. The most disastrous result of the proceedings was possibly a broken chair, which my husband threw into the kitchen by way of informing the cook that good news had come. Then I was tossed about the room, and all sorts of jokes were played upon me before the frolic was ended. After such celebration, I was almost too tired with the laughter and fun to begin packing. But we rushed through the one day given us for preparation, and I had only time to be glad with my husband that he was going back to the life of activity that he so loved.

In the confusion, I managed to retire to a corner with an atlas and look up the territory to which we were going. I hardly liked to own that I had forgotten its location. When my finger traced our route from Kentucky almost up to the border of the British Possessions [Canada], it seemed as if we were going to Lapland. Had I dared to stop and think of myself, all the courage would have gone out of me. This removal to Dakota Territory meant to my husband a reunion with his regiment and summer campaigns against Indians. But to me, it meant months of loneliness, anxiety, and terror. Fortunately there was too much to do to leave leisure for thought.

Steamers were ready for us at Memphis, Tennessee, and we went thither by rail to embark. When the regiment was gathered together, after a separation of two years, there were hearty greetings. Thankful once more to be reunited, we entered again, heart and soul, into the minutest detail of one another's lives. Three steamers were loaded, and we went on to Cairo, Illinois, where we found the trains prepared to take us into Dakota.

There may have been eight or nine hundred soldiers and as many horses. The property of the companies —

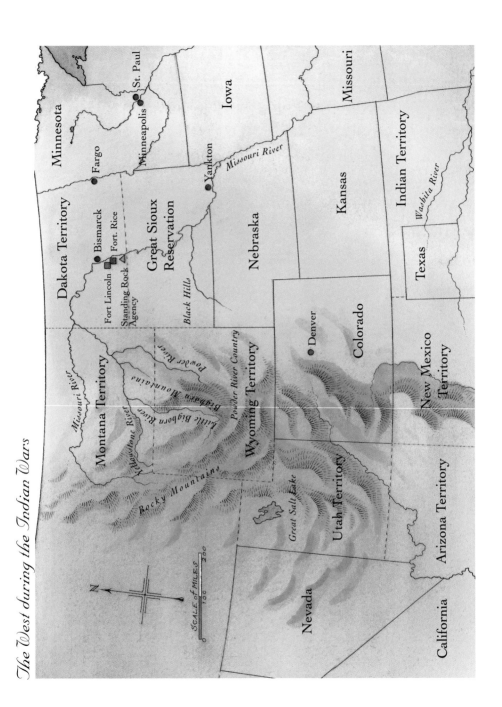

The West during the Indian Wars

Minnesota
St. Paul
Minneapolis
Fargo
Iowa
Missouri
Yankton
Missouri River
Dakota Territory
Bismarck
Fort Rice
Fort Lincoln
Standing Rock Agency
Great Sioux Reservation
Black Hills
Kansas
Indian Territory
Washita River
Nebraska
Texas
Missouri River
Montana Territory
Yellowstone River
Powder River
Little Bighorn River
Bighorn Mountains
Powder River Country
Wyoming Territory
Denver
Colorado
New Mexico Territory
Rocky Mountains
Great Salt Lake
Utah Territory
Nevada
Arizona Territory
California

N

SCALE OF MILES
0    100    200

saddles, equipments, arms, ammunition, and forage—together with the luggage of the officers, made the trains very heavy, and we traveled slowly. We were a week or more on the route.

# A Blizzard in April

After so many days in the [railroad] car, we were glad to stop on an open plain about a mile from the town of Yankton, in Dakota Territory, where the railroad ended. The long trains were unloaded of their freight, and the plains about us seemed to swarm with men and horses. The other ladies of the regiment went on to the hotel in the town. The general suggested that I go with them. But I had been in camp so many summers that it was not a formidable matter for me to remain, and fortunately for what followed I did so. The household belongings were gathered together. A family of little new puppies, some half-grown dogs, the cages of mockingbirds and canaries, were all corralled safely in a little stockade made of chests and trunks. The general and a number of soldiers were obliged to go at once to lay out the main camp. Later on, when the most important work was done, our tents were to be pitched. While I sat on a chest waiting, the air grew suddenly chilly, the bright sun of the morning disappeared, and the rain began to fall. Had we been accustomed to the climate, we would have known that these changes were the precursors of a snowstorm.

It seemed impossible that even so far north there could be a return to winter in the middle of April. But each new country has its peculiarities, and it seemed we had reached one where all the others were outdone. As the afternoon advanced, the wind blew colder, and I found myself eyeing with envy a little half-finished cabin, standing by itself. Some of the kindhearted soldiers found the owner, and he rented it to us for a few days. The place was equal to a palace to me.

Meanwhile, the general had returned completely exhausted and very ill. I sent for the surgeon, who gave me some powerful medicine to administer and forbade the general to leave his bed. It was growing dark, and we were now in the midst of a Dakota blizzard. The snow was fluffy and thick, like wool, and fell so rapidly, and seemingly from all directions, that it gave me a feeling of suffocation as I stood outside.

The night had almost settled down upon us when the general ordered the breaking of camp. All the soldiers were to take their horses and go into Yankton and ask the citizens to give them shelter in their homes, cowsheds, and stables. In a short time, the camp was nearly deserted. The black night closed in and left us alone on that wide, deserted plain. The wind grew higher and higher and shrieked about the little house dismally. Our servants, Mary and Ham, did what they could to make the cabin comfortable. But the thirty-six hours of our imprisonment there seems now a frightful nightmare.

During the night I was startled by a dull sound, as of something falling heavily. I found the servants prying open the snow-packed door, to admit a half-dozen soldiers, who had been saved by the faint light we had placed in the window. One of the soldiers explained that they had attempted to find their way to town, but the storm had completely overcome them. After that several more came, and two were badly frozen. Poor fellows! They afterwards lost their feet, and some of their fingers had also to be amputated.

At last the day came, but so darkened by snow that it seemed rather a twilight. The long hours dragged themselves away, leaving the general too weak to rise. The snow continued to come down in great, swirling sheets. When night came again and the cold increased, I believed that our hours were numbered.

During the night the sound of the tramping of many feet rose above the roar of the storm. A great drove of mules rushed up to the sheltered side of the house. Their brays had a sound of terror as they pushed, kicked, and crowded themselves against our little cabin. For a time they huddled together, hoping for warmth, and then despairing, they made a mad rush away and were soon lost in the white wall of snow. All night long, the neigh of a distressed horse, almost human in its appeal, came to us at intervals. Occasionally a lost dog lifted up a howl under our window, but before the door could be opened for him, he had disappeared in the darkness. No one, until he hears it for himself, can realize what sounds animals make when in peril.

Every minute seemed a day, every hour a year. It was almost unbearable to hear the groans of the soldiers over their swollen and painful feet and know that we could do nothing to ease them. When daylight came again, I dropped into an exhausted slumber and was awakened by Mary standing over our bed with a tray of hot breakfast. The breakfast revived the general so much that he began to make light of danger in order to quiet me. The snow had ceased to fall, but it still seemed that we were castaways and forgotten, hidden under the drifts that surrounded us.

Help was really near at hand, however, at this darkest hour. A knock at the door, and the cheery voices of men came to our ears. Some citizens of Yankton had at last found their way to us, and the officers, who neither knew the way nor how to travel over such a country, had gladly followed. Some of the officers had brought parcels containing food, while our brother, Colonel Tom Custer, had struggled with a large basket of supplies. Paths and roads were made through the snow, and it was a great relief to be again in the scenes of busy life.

Now we understood why the frontiersman builds his stable near the house and why he does not dare to cross in a blizzard from the house to the stable door without keeping hold of a rope tied fast to the latch. We did not soon forget our introduction to Dakota.

# Storms, Cactus Thorns, and Rattlesnakes

When the day came for us to begin our march to Fort Rice, near the town of Bismarck, in Dakota Territory, the sun shone and the townspeople of Yankton wished us good luck with their good-bye.

At the bugle call "Boots and Saddles," each soldier mounted and took his place in line, all riding two abreast. As usual, I rode beside the general. The general's sister Margaret made her first march with her husband, Lieutenant James Calhoun, riding all the way on horseback. Then came the companies, according to the places assigned them for the day, and finally the wagon train, with the rear guard. We made a long, drawn-out cavalcade that stretched over a great distance. When we reached some high bluff, we never tired of watching the command advancing, with the long line of supply wagons, with their white covers, winding around bends in the road and climbing over the hills.

We had a citizen guide with us, who, having been long in the country, knew the streams. The general and I, following his instructions, often rode in advance as we neared the night's camp.

An ineffaceable picture remains with me even now of those lovely camps, as we dreamily watched them by the fading light of the afternoon. The general and I used to think there was no bit of color equal to the delicate blue line of smoke which rose from the campfire, where the soldiers' suppers were being cooked. The mellow air brought us sounds that had become dear by long and happy association—the low notes of the bugle, the click of the currycomb as soldiers groomed their horses, the whistle or song of a happy trooper. And even the irrepressible accordion at that distance made a melody.

The twilight almost always found many of us gathered together, some idling on the grass in front of the campfire, or lounging on buffalo robes. The one with the best voice sang, while all joined in the chorus.

As we went farther north, the twilights became longer, and I was greatly deceived by having so much daylight. Storms came down in great belts of rain sometimes, and if the country were level enough we could look ahead on the plain and see where the storm was crossing. This enabled us to halt in time to escape a sheet of pouring rain which fell like a wall of water directly before us.

The dogs had almost as hard a time becoming accustomed to the Dakota climate as we did. In addition, we had to be their nurses and surgeons. One of the dogs was called "Lucy Stone." I can see her now, sitting deliberately down in the road directly in front of us and

*The general and I used to think there was no bit of color equal to the delicate blue line of smoke which rose from the campfire.*

holding up a paw full of cactus thorns. Her howls and upturned eyes meant an appeal, certainly. Her master would leap to the ground, sit down in the road, and taking the old creature in his arms, begin the surgery. With tweezers he worked tenderly and long to extract the tormenting cactus needles. So it often happened that my traveling wagon was the hospital for an ill or footsore dog.

It was of no use to try to keep the dogs out of my tent. If it were very cold, I found dogs under and on the camp bed and so thickly scattered over the floor that I had to step carefully over them to avoid hurting feet or tails. If I secured a place in the bed, I was fortunate. Sometimes, when it had rained and all of them were wet, I rebelled. The steam from their shaggy coats was stifling, but the general begged so hard for them that I taught myself to endure the air at last. My favorite dog was a cream-colored staghound named "Cardigan." He was enormous, yet he never gave up trying to be my lap dog.

The rattlesnakes were so numerous on this march that all my Texas and Kansas experience seemed to dwarf in contrast. My horse was over sixteen hands high, but I would gladly have exchanged him for a camelopard* when I rode suddenly upon a snake coiled in the grass and looked down into the eyes of the upraised head. The men became expert in clearing the camp of these reptiles.

*camelopard—an old term for "giraffe"

If we halted at night in the underbrush, they cut and tore away the reeds and grass and began at once to beat the ground and kill the snakes. We counted those we encountered in one day's journey until we were tired. When I say that as many as forty were killed in one night, it is not an exaggerated story.

# Camping among the Sioux: Fool-Dog and Two Bears

Most of our march took us through the Indian Reservations, grounds set apart by the Government for the use of the Sioux who were at peace with our country. We had not made much progress before we began to see their graves. They do not bury their dead, but place them on boards lashed to the limbs of trees, or on high platforms raised from the ground. The body is wound round and round with clothing or blankets, like a mummy, and inside the layers are placed firearms, tobacco, and jerked beef, to supply them on the imaginary journey to the happy hunting-grounds. In the early morning when it was not quite light, we filed by these solitary sepulchers. It was uncanny and weird, and the sun, when it came, was doubly welcome.

Our first visitor from agency Indians was Fool-Dog, a Sioux chief. He was tall, commanding, and had really a fine face. He invited us to come to his village before we left on our next march. At twilight my husband and I walked over. The village was a collection of tepees of all sizes, the largest being the Medicine Lodge, where the councils are held. It was formed of tanned buffalo hides, stretched over a collection of poles. Around this lodge were more poles, from which were suspended rags. In these were their medicines of roots and herbs to keep off evil spirits. The sound of music came from within; I crept tremblingly in after the general and sat on the buffalo robe beside him. I knew how resolute the Indians were in never admitting women to council, and their curious eyes and forbidding expressions toward me did not add to my comfort. The dust, smoke, and noise in the fading light were not reassuring, either. Fool-Dog arose from the circle and solemnly shook hands with the general. The pipe was then smoked, and the general had to take a whiff when it came his turn.

How relieved I felt when the final pipe was smoked and the good-bye said! The curious eyes of the squaws, who stood in the vicinity of the lodge, followed us as we disappeared in the direction of camp, through the thickening gloom.

As we approached more villages, the chiefs usually came out to receive us. There were many high-sounding words of welcome, translated by our guide, who, having lived among Indians for many years, knew the different dialects.

A Sioux chief called Two Bears had the most picturesque village that we saw. The lodges were placed in a circle; the ponies were herded inside the enclosure at night. This precaution was necessary, for the neighboring tribes swept down on them after dark and ran off the stock if they were not secured.

*The village was a collection of tepees of all sizes, the largest being the Medicine Lodge, where the councils are held.*

# INDIAN RESERVATIONS

The United States government, faced with the post-Civil War expansion in industry and population, decided that it could not allow Native Americans to keep control of millions of acres of land in the West. In 1869 President Ulysses S. Grant formulated his "Peace Policy." Its aim was to complete, without bloodshed, the process that had begun in the previous century—settling all of America's Indians onto reservations.

The government's treaty of 1868 had already set aside an area in the northern plains called the Great Sioux Reservation. It included about 43,000 square miles in southwestern Dakota Territory and was further divided into six separate "agencies," to accommodate different Plains tribes. The treaty also promised the Sioux and Cheyenne complete control of the Powder River Country; it was to remain off-limits to whites forever.

But the government did not honor all the provisions of the treaty of 1868, and Grant's Peace Policy soon dissolved into violence. Indians on the reservations were poor and hungry, living on meager government handouts. They frequently "broke out" and traveled west to the Powder River Country to visit the remaining bands of free Indians and to hunt the few buffalo left on the plains. The army often could not tell the difference between the "friendlies," or reservation people, and the independent "hostiles."

In a strange way, General Custer himself sympathized with the "hostiles," even while he fought them: "If I were an Indian, I would greatly prefer to cast my lot among those of my people who adhered to the free open plains rather than submit to the confined limits of a reservation."

Just outside this village, the chiefs sat in a circle awaiting us. Two Bears, a dignified old man wrapped in his blanket, arose to welcome the general and asked him to go with him to his lodge. I was asked to go also, and we dipped our heads and crept into the tepee. There we also met Two Bears' daughter. Her feet were in moccasins, her legs and ankles wound round with beaded leggings, and she had on the one buckskin garment which never varies in cut through all the tribes. A blanket drawn over her head was belted at her waist. To crown all this, she had an open parasol, brought to her, doubtless, as a present by some Indian returning from a council at Washington.

When we returned to the outer entrance of the village, the whole tribe was assembled and attired in gala dress in our honor. There were but few young men. Their absence was always excused by the same reason—they were out hunting. But we knew how little game there was; an occasional jackrabbit, some plover, and a few wild ducks were all that were left. We surmised—what we after-wards found to be true—that the young men had joined the hostile tribes and only came in to the reservation for the distribution of supplies and presents in the fall.

# Danger in the Cottonwoods

My husband and I kept up our little detours by ourselves as we neared the hour for camping each day. One day one of the officers accompanied us. We left the higher ground to go down by the water to wander through the cottonwood trees that fringed the river for several miles. As usual, we had a number of dogs leaping and racing around us. Two of them started a deer, and the general bounded after them, encouraging the others with his voice to follow. He had left his friend with me, and we rode leisurely along to see that the younger dogs did not get lost. Without the least warning, in the dead stillness of that desolate spot, we suddenly came upon a group of young Indian warriors seated in their motionless way in the underbrush. I became cold and numb with terror.

The Indians snatched up their guns, leaped upon their ponies, and prepared for attack. The officer with me was perfectly calm, spoke to them coolly without a change of voice, and rode quickly beside me, telling me to advance. My horse reared violently and started to run. The general was just visible ascending a bluff beyond. To avoid showing fear when every nerve is strung to its utmost and your heart leaps into your throat requires superhuman effort. I managed to check my horse and did not scream. No amount of telling over to myself what I had been told, that all the tribes on this side of the Missouri River were peaceable and that only those on the other side were warlike, could quell the throbbing of my pulses. I knew well that it was a matter of no time for warriors to cross the water on their little tublike boats that shoot madly down the tide.

Whether because of the coolness of the officer, or because the warriors knew of the size of the advancing column of cavalry, we were allowed to proceed unharmed. How interminable the distance seemed to where the general awaited us, unconscious of what we had encountered!

The next day the general thought I might rather not go with him than run the risk of such frights, but I well knew there was something far worse than fears for my own personal safety. It is worse to be left behind, a prey to imagining what may be happening to one we love. You eat your heart slowly out with anxiety, and to endure such suspense is the hardest of all trials that come to the soldier's wife.

During the last days of our march, we came upon another warning from the Indians. Stuck in the trail before us was a pole with a red flag, to which were fastened locks of hair. It was a challenge that meant that if we persisted in advancing, the hostiles were ready to meet the soldiers and fight them. The officers paid little attention to this, but my heart was like lead for days afterwards.

We encamped that night near what the Indians call "Medicine Rock," and my husband and I walked out to see it. It was a large stone, showing on the flat surface the impress of hands and feet made ages ago, before the clay was petrified. The Indians had tied bags of their herb medicine on poles about the rock. Tin cans, spoons, and forks that they had bought at the agency on account of the brightness of the metal were also left there as offerings to an unseen God.

Everything pertaining to the Indians was new and interesting to me. While we were in Kansas the tribes were at war, and we had not the opportunity to see their daily life as we did while passing through the Sioux reservations on the march.

I regretted each day that brought us nearer the conclusion of our journey, for though I had been frightened by Indians, and though we had encountered cold, storms, and rough life, the pleasures of the trip overbalanced the discomforts.

# Separation and Reunion

The day at last came for our march of five hundred miles to terminate. A rickety old ferryboat that took us over the river made a halt near Fort Rice, and there we established ourselves. Strange to say, the Missouri River was no narrower there than it was so many hundred miles below, where we had started. Muddy and full of sandbars as the river was, we began bravely to drink its water and to take our bath in what at first seemed liquid mud.

All thought began now to center on the coming events of the summer. The regiment was to go out to guard the engineers of the Northern Pacific Railroad while they surveyed the route from Bismarck to the Yellowstone River. The ladies were to be left behind.

Now began the summer of my discontent. I longed to remain in Dakota, for I knew it would take much longer for letters to reach me if I went East. I was willing to live in a tent alone at the post, but there were not even tents to be had. There was nothing left for sister Margaret and me but to go home to Monroe, Michigan. It was a sore disappointment. For several slow, irksome months, I did little else than wait for the tardy mails and count each day that passed.

When the expedition returned from the Yellowstone, a dispatch came to me in Michigan, saying the regiment

# THE YELLOWSTONE EXPEDITION

The Yellowstone Expedition set out with railroad surveyors, scouts, about fifteen hundred soldiers, and almost three hundred covered wagons. It snaked along the path of the Yellowstone River in order to survey the region for the building of the Northern Pacific Railroad as it inched into Montana Territory. Amid the grasslands and the bluffs carved out by the river, Custer and his men had their first encounters with Crazy Horse and his warriors. In one fight, Custer's horse was shot from under him, but he and all but a few members of the expedition escaped with their lives.

Libbie might have complained about the "tardy mails," but when letters arrived, they were full of news and descriptions. His clashes with Crazy Horse had not kept Autie from admiring the beauty of the Yellowstone country. It was "almost like another world," he wrote, a "Wonderland!"

had reached Fort Lincoln in safety. Another soon followed, informing me that my husband was on his way to Michigan. There was to be an army reunion in the city nearest us. In my impatience, I took the first train, thinking to reach there before General Custer. As I walked along the street, looking into shop windows, I felt a sudden rush from a door, and I was taken off my feet and set dancing in air. Before I could resent what I thought was an indignity, I discovered that it was my husband. He was sunburned and mottled, for the flesh was quite fair where he had cut his beard, the growth of the summer. He told me the officers with whom he had traveled in the Pullman car had teased him and declared that no man would shave in a car going at forty miles an hour, except to prepare to meet his sweetheart.

The general was at this time thirty-five years of age, weighed one hundred and seventy pounds, and was nearly six feet in height. His eyes were clear blue, his hair wavy and golden in tint. He was the most agile, active man I ever knew, and it was always a delight to see him ride. Horse and man seemed one when he vaulted into the saddle. His body was so lightly poised and so full of swinging motion, it almost seemed that the wind moved him as it blew over the plain. He was a figure that would have fixed attention anywhere.

# Fort Abraham Lincoln, "Home, Sweet Home"

In a few days we were ready to return to Dakota and very glad to go, except for leaving the old parents. The hardest trial of my husband's life was parting with his mother.

When we finally reached the termination of the railroad at Bismarck, the street was full of people, wildly expostulating and talking loudly and fiercely. Another train was starting back to St. Paul. It appeared to be the last train of the season, as the cars were not to run during the winter. Its passengers were mostly Bismarck citizens, whose lawless life as gamblers and murderers had so outraged the few law-abiding residents that they had forced them to depart. We could see these outlaws crowding at the door, hanging out of the windows, swearing and menacing, and finally firing on the crowd as the cars passed out of town. We quietly slipped out on the other side of the depot and were driven to the river, which had to be crossed in a small boat.

Our brother, Colonel Tom, met us and drove us to our new home. In the dim light, I could see the great post of Fort Lincoln, where only a few months before we had left a barren plain. As we approached, the regimental

*We could see these outlaws crowding at the door, hanging out of the windows, swearing and menacing, and finally firing on the crowd.*

band played "Home, Sweet Home," followed by the general's favorite song, "Garryowen."

The general had completely settled our house before he left for Michigan, but he had kept this fact secret, as a surprise. Our friends had lighted it all and built fires in the fireplaces. The garrison had gathered to welcome us, and Mary had a grand supper ready.

Fort Lincoln was located in a valley, while just back of us stretched a long chain of bluffs. The post was built with quarters for six companies. The barracks for the soldiers were on the side of the parade ground, nearest the river, while seven detached houses for officers faced the river opposite. Outside the garrison proper, near the river, were the stables for six hundred horses. Still farther beyond were the quarters for the laundresses, dubbed "Suds Row." Some distance on from there were the log huts of the Indian scouts and their families. On the left of the post was the sutler's store, with a billiard room attached. Soon after the general arrived, he permitted a citizen to put up a barber shop, and afterwards another built a little cabin for a photographer's establishment. It seemed too good to believe that the 7th Cavalry had a post of its own.

# The Burning of Our Quarters

We had hardly finished arranging our quarters when one freezing night I was awakened by a roaring sound in a chimney that had been defective from the first. The sound grew too loud to be mistaken, and I awakened my husband. He ran upstairs and found the room above us on fire. He called to me to bring him some water, believing he could extinguish it himself. While I hurried after the water, there came such a crash and explosion that my brain seemed to reel from fright. I had no thought but that my husband was killed. Nothing can describe the relief with which I heard his voice calling. His escape was very narrow. The chimney had burst, the whole side of the room was blown out, and he was covered with plaster and surrounded with fallen bricks.

In an incredibly short time, men were swarming about the house. I ran in my nightdress over the snow to our sister's. The house burned very quickly. Fortunately it was a still, cold night, and there was no wind to spread the flames. Except for this, the whole garrison must have burned.

When the morning came, we went to inspect the heap of household belongings that had been carried out on the parade ground. It was a sorry collection of torn, broken, and marred effects! Most of my clothes were gone. The only loss I mourned, as it was really irreparable, was a collection of newspaper clippings regarding my husband that I had saved during and since the war.

The general selected another set of quarters next to his brother's and thither removed the remnants of our household goods. He begged me not to go near this house, or attempt to settle, until I had recovered from the fright of the fire.

The second evening after the fire, he sent for me and asked if I would come and consult with him about some arrangement of the furniture. I went to the new house to find the band playing "Home, Sweet Home." To my utter surprise, I found the whole place completely settled and the garrison assembled at the general's invitation for a housewarming. Everyone tried by merry frolic and dancing to make me forget the catastrophe, and the general, bubbling over with fun, inspired me to join. Then he told me to what subterfuges he had resorted to get the house ready and repeated to me again that it was never worthwhile to "cry over spilled milk."

# A Day of Anxiety and Terror

When the air became milder, it was a delight to be able to dawdle on the piazza*. The valley below us was beginning to show a tinge of verdure. Several hundred mules belonging to the supply wagon train dotted the turf and nibbled as best they could the sprouting grass. Half a dozen mule herders lounged on the sod, sleepily guarding the herd. One morning we were walking back and forth, looking down the long, level plain, when we were startled by shouts. A hatless and breathless herder dashed up on an unsaddled mule. With blanched face and protruding eyeballs, he called out that the Indians were running off the herd.

The general came hastily out, just in time to see a cloud of dust rising through a gap in the bluffs, marking the direction taken by the stampeded mules. He shouted to the bugler to sound the call "Boots and Saddles." The first notes of the trumpet had hardly sounded before everyone rushed from the barracks and officers' quarters to the stables. The men threw their saddles on their horses and galloped out to the parade ground. Finding the reason for the hasty summons when they all gathered together, they could hardly brook even a few moments' delay.

*piazza — the porch of a house

The general stopped to caution me not to go outside the post, and with a hasty good-bye, flung himself into the saddle and was off. The command spurred their horses toward the opening in the bluff, through which the last mules had passed. In twenty minutes the garrison was emptied, and we women stood watching the cloud of dust that the horses had stirred as they hurled themselves through the cleft in the hills.

We had hardly collected our senses before we found that we were almost deserted. We realized that, in addition to our anxiety for those who had just left us, we were in peril ourselves. Though Indians rarely attack a post directly, the pickets* that were stationed on the low hills at the rear of the garrison had been fired upon previously. We also feared that the buildings would be set on fire.

The Custer house being the last in the line and commanding an extended view of the valley, we officers' wives kept our lookout there. Each of us took turns mounting the porch railing and fixing the field glass on the little spot of earth through which the command had vanished. And so that long day dragged away. About five o'clock in the afternoon, the mules appeared, traveling wearily back through the same opening in the bluffs through which so many hours before they had rushed headlong. We were bitterly disappointed to find only a few soldiers driving them; the rest of the command had

*pickets —soldiers assigned to watch for danger

pushed on in pursuit of the Indians. The night set in as we scanned the horizon, and still we were in suspense.

From this miserable frame of mind we were thrown into a new excitement, but fortunately not out of fear: We heard the sound of the band ringing out on the still evening air. From an entirely different direction from that in which they had left, the regiment appeared, marching to the familiar notes of "Garryowen." Such a welcome as met them! The relief from the anxiety of that day was inexpressible.

When the herders were questioned next day, it was found that the Indians had started the stampede by riding suddenly up from the river, where they had been concealed. Uttering the wildest yells, they each swung a buffalo robe about the ears of the easily excited mules.

The regiment had ridden twenty miles out, as hard as the speed of the horses would allow. The general and one other officer, mounted like himself on a Kentucky thoroughbred, found themselves far in advance and almost up to some of the Indians. But the Sioux threw themselves from their ponies and plunged into the underbrush of a deep ravine where no horse could follow. The ponies were captured, but it was useless to try any further pursuit.

# The Summer of the
# Black Hills Expedition

I used to be thankful that ours was a mounted regiment on one account: If we had belonged to the infantry, the regiment would have been sent out much sooner. The horses were too valuable to have their lives endangered by encountering a blizzard, while it was believed that an enlisted man had enough pluck and endurance to bring him out of a storm in one way or another. The grass began at last to be suitable for grazing, and preparations for an expedition to the Black Hills were being carried on. I had found accidentally that my husband was fitting up an ambulance for traveling, and as he never rode in one himself, I decided at once that he was planning to take me with him. At the very last, news came through Indian scouts that the summer might be full of danger, and my heart was almost broken at finding that the general did not dare to take me.

The black hour came again and with it the terrible parting. When I resumed my life and tried to portion off the day with occupations in order that the time should fly faster, I found that the one silver thread running through the dragging hours was the hope of the letters we were

# EXPLORING THE BLACK HILLS

The Black Hills were a refuge and a sacred place to the Plains Indians. Pa Sapa, as the Sioux called the area, was also part of the Great Sioux Reservation. Whites were forbidden to enter. So Custer, along with the United States Army, was in violation of the treaty of 1868 when he led the expedition there in 1874.

The Seventh Cavalry was accompanied by photographers, reporters, scientists, and a long line of covered wagons pulled by teams of mules. The Black Hills were magical, Custer found, as he explored mountains and pine forests, waterfalls and flower-splashed meadows. "One of the most beautiful spots on God's green earth," wrote another man.

Soon after entering Pa Sapa, miners on the expedition found gold glinting in a creek. When Custer's men returned with this news to their fort, a gold rush began in the Indians' holy place. The government tried hard to buy the Black Hills from the Sioux, but many of them agreed with Crazy Horse: "One does not sell the earth upon which the people walk." President Grant blamed the free Powder River Indians for this refusal to sell. In 1875 he ordered them all to the reservations. A showdown was unavoidable now.

promised. Scouts were to be sent back four times during the absence of the regiment.

The sun burns fiercely during the short Northern summer. With the hot weather the mosquito war began — Fort Lincoln was celebrated as the worst place in the United States for these pests. If the wind was in a certain direction, they tormented us all day long. It required constant activity to keep off the swarms of those wretched little insects that annoyed us every moment. In the evening we became almost desperate. It seemed very hard, after our long winter's imprisonment, to miss a single hour out-of-doors during the short summer.

So every evening, we officers' wives assembled on the wide piazza of our house. We were obliged to make special preparations for our protection, and they were far from becoming. Someone discovered that wrapping newspapers around our ankles and feet, and drawing the stocking over, would protect down to the slipper. Then, after tucking our skirts closely around us, we fixed ourselves in a chair, not daring to move. I had adopted a head net and added a waterproof cloak, buckskin gauntlets, and the general's riding-boots! Tucked up like a mummy, I was something at which no one could resist laughing.

The cattle and horses suffered pitiably during the reign of the mosquitoes. They used to push their way into the underbrush to try if a thicket would afford them protection.

*Someone discovered that wrapping newspapers around our ankles and feet, and drawing the stockings over, would protect down to the slipper.*

The cattle grew thin, for there were days when it was impossible for them to graze. We knew of their being driven mad and dying of exhaustion after a long season of torment. The poor dogs dug deep holes in the side of the hills, where they half smothered in their attempt to escape.

We knew that we could not expect in that climate that the freshness of summer would last for more than a short time after the sun had come to its supremest in the way of heat. That year even our brief enjoyment of the verdure was cut short. One day the sky became copper colored and the air murky and stifling. A sirocco came up suddenly. This wind, so strong that it seemed to shrivel the skin, lasted for two hours. After that, no green thing was left. The grass was burned down into the roots, and when we walked, our shoes were cut by the crisp, brown stubble. As far as we could see, the scorched earth sent up over its surface floating waves of heated atmosphere. The only flowers that had not been scorched out of existence were the soap plants, which have roots that extend for many feet in all directions, and the bluebell, which dotted a hill where we were accustomed to climb. One can scarcely imagine how hungrily we gazed at those little blossoms in that stripped and almost "God-forgotten" land.

Our eyes seemed to be perpetually strained, watching the horizon for the scouts bringing our letters, which had been unfortunately delayed. At dawn one morning—which is at three o'clock in summer in Dakota—I was awakened by strange sounds at the door. There were the Ree scouts, and on their ponies the mailbag, marked by some joking soldier, "Black Hills Express." It took but a second for me to fling on a wrapper and fairly tumble down the steps. The Indians made the sign of "Long Hair," which is a name the general had borne with them for some time. Soon the great official envelope, crowded with his closely written pages, was in my hand. Three times after that we had letters. They were most interesting, with descriptions of the charm of traveling over ground no white feet had ever before touched.

When the day of the expedition's return came, I was wild with joy. When we wives took time to look the men over, we were amused enough. Many, like the general, had grown heavy beards. All were sunburned, their hair faded, and their clothes so patched that the original blue of the uniform was scarcely visible.

By and by the long wagon train appeared. Many of the covers had elk horns strapped to them, until they looked like strange, bristling animals as they drew near. Some of the antlers were brought to us as presents. Besides them we had skins, specimens of gold and mica, and petrified shells of iridescent colors, snake rattles, pressed flowers, and petrified wood. My husband brought me a keg of the most delicious water from a mountain stream. It was almost my only look at clear water for years, as most of the streams west of the Missouri are muddy.

From the clouds and gloom of those summer days, I walked again into the broad blaze of sunshine which my husband's blithe spirit made. I did everything I could to put out of my mind the long, anxious, lonely months.

# Capture and Escape of Rain-in-the-Face

As the second winter progressed, it bade fair to be a repetition of the first, until an event happened that excited us all very much.

I must preface my account of the occurrence by going back to the summer of the Yellowstone campaign, in 1873. Two of the citizens attached to the expedition, one as the sutler, the other as the veterinary surgeon, were in the habit of riding by themselves a great deal. Not being enlisted men, much more liberty than soldiers have was allowed them. Many warnings were given, however, and an instance, fresh in the minds of the officers, of the killing by Indians of two of their comrades the year before was repeatedly told to them. One day their last hour of lingering came. While they stopped to water their horses, some Indians concealed in a gully shot them within sight of our regiment, who were then fighting on the hill. Both of the murdered men were favorites. Both left families, and regret and sympathy were general throughout the command.

A year and a half afterwards, information came to our post, Fort Lincoln, that an Indian was then at the agency at Standing Rock, boasting of the murder of these two men. A detachment of two officers and a hundred men was quickly prepared. It started out with orders to capture and bring back an Uncapapa Indian called Rain-in-the-Face, the avowed murderer of the sutler and the veterinary surgeon. The general had selected his brother Tom to assist in this delicate transaction, as he had been wont to do ever since they began their life of adventure together during the war. The detachment arrived on the day that the Indians were drawing their rations of beef. There were five hundred Sioux at the agency, armed with the latest long-range rifles.

Colonel Tom Custer was ordered to take five men and go to the trader's store, where the Indians resort constantly. There at last he saw Rain-in-the-Face. Coming suddenly from behind, Tom threw his arms about him and seized the Indian's Winchester rifle. Rain-in-the-Face was taken entirely by surprise. He drew himself up in an independent manner, to show his brother warriors that he did not dread death.

After the command had returned and the officers had reported, General Custer sent for Rain-in-the-Face. He was tall, straight, and young. His face was quite imperturbable. He gave a brief account of the murders, saying that neither man was scalped, as the elder was bald and the younger had closely cropped hair. The next day he made a full confession before all the officers. This cruel story set their blood flowing hotly, and it is not to be wondered at that each officer strode out of the room with blazing eyes.

Two Indians, one of them Iron Horse, the prisoner's brother, had followed the cavalry up from the agency and asked to see their comrade. The general sent again for Rain-in-the-Face, who came into the room with clanking chains and with the guard at his heels. Iron Horse supposed that he was to be hanged at once, and that this would be the final interview.

It was an impressive and melancholy scene. Iron Horse charged his brother not to attempt to escape, saying, that if he did get back to the reservation he would surely be recaptured. Perhaps the white chief would intercede for him to obtain his pardon. After asking him not to lose courage, Iron Horse smoked with his brother and silently withdrew. In about ten days Iron Horse returned, bringing a portion of his tribe with him.

The valley of the Missouri River is wide and slopes gradually back to the bluffs. Beyond are the plains, rolling away for hundreds of miles to another river. There was a level stretch of three miles below our post, and from this direction we watched the approach of the bands of Indians coming from the reservation. We could see their arms glistening far down the valley. Every available bit of metal that could catch the light reflected and shone in the morning sun. As the bands came nearer, the sun caught a bit of gaudy scarlet or touched for a moment one of the feathers in a war bonnet.

The war bonnets, shields, and necklaces of bears' claws are all handed down from faraway grandfathers and only aired on grand occasions. The Indians had many weapons, all kept in a brilliant and glistening state. The tomahawk is one of the heirlooms of the collection of arms. The knife, pistol, and rifle are very modern and are always kept in the most perfect condition.

The Indians with Iron Horse asked for a council, so as many as could get into the general's room entered. Iron Horse wore an elaborately beaded and painted buckskin shirt, with solid embroidery of porcupine quills. His sleeves and shoulders were ornamented with a fringe of scalp locks. The chief of the tribe wore on his shoulders a sort of cape, trimmed with snowy ermine. His hair was wound round and round with strips of otter that hung down his back, and his scalp-lock was also tightly wound. Three eagle feathers, denoting the number of warriors killed, were so fastened to the lock that they stood erect. There were perforations in each ear from which depended bead earrings, and thrown around him was a beaded blanket. The costumes were simply superb.

The Indians took their places according to rank in a semicircle about the general. The pipe was filled and lighted. After all in the first circle had smoked a little, the general included, they passed the pipe back through each warrior's hand to the chief. When the pipe was finally put away, the Indians asked to have Rain-in-the-Face present. He came into the room, trying to hide his pleasure at seeing his friends and his grief at his imprisonment.

Iron Horse began his speech, asking that the Great Father [President Ulysses S. Grant] in Washington spare his brother's life. He then slowly took off his buckskin shirt and presented it to my husband. After all the ranking Indians had followed Iron Horse in speeches, the pipe was again produced. When it was smoked, the whole band filed out to eat the presents of food the general had given them and soon afterwards disappeared down the valley on their way home.

Rain-in-the-Face occupied a part of the guardhouse with a citizen who had been caught stealing grain from the storehouse. For several months they had been chained together. After a time, the citizen, with help from his friends outside, cut a hole in the wall at night and escaped. He broke the chain attaching him to the Indian, who was left free to follow. We found afterwards that Rain-in-the-Face did not dare to return to the reservation, but made his way to the hostile camp. In the spring of 1875 he sent word from there by an agency Indian that he had joined Sitting Bull and was awaiting his revenge for his imprisonment.

# Running Antelope Tells of Hunger

The Indians came several times from the reservations for counsel, but the occasion that made the greatest impression upon me was towards the spring. They came to implore the general for food. In the fall, the steamer bringing them supplies had been detained in starting. It had hardly accomplished half the required distance before the ice impeded its progress, and it lay out in the channel, frozen in, all winter. The suffering among the Indians was very great. They were compelled to eat their dogs and ponies to keep from starving. Believing a personal appeal would be effectual, they asked to come to our post for a council.

The Indian band brought their great orator Running Antelope. He was intensely dignified and fine looking. His face when he spoke was expressive. As he stood among them all in the general's room, he made an indelible impression on my memory. Running Antelope described the distressing condition of the tribe with real eloquence. But while he spoke, one of my husband's birds that was uncaged floated down and alighted on the warrior's head. It had been so petted, no ordinary movement startled the little thing. It maintained its balance, as the Indian moved his head in gesture. The orator saw that the faces of the other Indians showed signs of humor, but he was ignorant

*While Running Antelope spoke, one of my husband's birds floated down and alighted on the warrior's head.*

of what amused them. Finally the bird whirled up to its favorite resting place on the horn of a buffalo head, and the warrior understood the unusual sight of a smile from his people.

His appeal also touched the quick sympathies of my husband. Since the storehouses at our post were filled with supplies, he promised to telegraph to the Great Father for permission to give the Indians rations until spring. Not content with a complaint of their present wrongs, Running Antelope went off into an earnest denunciation of the agents, calling them dishonest.

The general interrupted and asked the interpreter to say that the Great Father selected the agents from among good men before sending them out from Washington. Running Antelope quickly responded, "They may be good men when they leave the Great Father, but they get to be cheats by the time they reach us."

The answer came next day from the Secretary of War that the Department of the Interior, which had the Indians in charge, refused to allow any army supplies to be distributed to the reservations. The chiefs were compelled to return to their reservations, where long ago all the game had been shot and their famishing tribesmen were increasingly driven to join the hostiles who followed Sitting Bull. We were not surprised that the warriors were discouraged and desperate, and that the raids on the settlements increased.

# A Wet Spring and the Last Peaceful Summer

The day of the final breaking up of the ice in the Missouri was one of great excitement to us. The roar and crash of the ice fields could be heard a great distance. The sound was the signal for the whole garrison to go out on the hill near the infantry post and watch the grand sight. Just above us was a bend in the river, and around this curve great floes of ice rushed, heaping up in huge masses as they swept down the furious current. All the lowlands that lay between Bismarck and the river were inundated, and the shore far in was covered with blocks of ice that the force of the water had thrown there.

Of all our happy days, the happiest had now come to us at Fort Lincoln. When the winter was finally gone there was not an hour that we would not have recalled. My husband used to tell me that he believed he was the happiest man on earth, and I cannot help thinking that he was. For with all the vicissitudes of those twelve eventful years, I never knew him to have an hour's depression. The presence of so many of his family about him was an unceasing pleasure. There was an abiding fondness between his brother, Colonel Tom, and himself. Tom always lived with us, and the brothers played incessant jokes on each other. The general once said to some Eastern friends, "To prove to you how I value and admire my brother as a soldier, I think that he should be the general and I the captain."

When spring came again, it is impossible to express the joy I felt that there was to be no summer campaign, and for the first time in many years, I saw the grass grow without a shudder. The general began the improvement of the post with fresh energy, and from the drill ground came the click of the horses' hoofs and the note of the bugles repeating the commands of the officers.

Almost our only exercise on summer evenings was walking on the outskirts of the garrison, surrounded by the dogs. It was dangerous to go far, but we could walk with safety in the direction of the huts of the Indian scouts. Their life always interested us, and by degrees they became so accustomed to our presence that they went on with all their occupations without heeding us.

There was a variety of articles in front of these Indian quarters. Lariats, saddles, and worn-out robes were heaped about their *travois*, arrangements for conveying their property from place to place. Some of their boats lay upturned about the door. These were round, like a great bowl, and composed of a wicker frame over which buffalo hide was tightly drawn. They seemed barely large enough to hold two Indians, who were obliged to crouch down as they paddled their way with short, awkward oars through the rapid current of the Missouri.

At Indian quarters, the general often had long interviews with Bloody Knife, who had proved himself such an invaluable scout. Seated on the grass, the dogs lying about them, they talked over portions of the country that the general had never seen, the scout drawing excellent maps in the sand with a pointed stick. He was often moody, and it required the utmost patience on my husband's part to submit to his humors. But Bloody Knife's fidelity and cleverness made it worthwhile to yield to his tempers.

As the soldiers and citizens all knew the general's love of pets, we had constant presents. Many of them I would have gladly declined, but notwithstanding, a badger, porcupine, raccoon, prairie dog, and wild turkey, all served their brief time as members of our family. They were comparatively harmless, and I had only the inconvenience to encounter. But when a ferocious wildcat was brought in, I was inclined to mutiny. My husband made allowance for my dread of the creature and decided to send him into the States as a present to one of the zoological gardens, for in its way it was a treasure.

At one time the general tamed a tiny field mouse and kept it in a large, empty inkstand on his desk. It grew very fond of him and ran over his head and shoulders and even through his hair. The general, thinking at last that it was cruel to detain the little thing indoors when it belonged by nature to the fields, took it out and left it on the plain. The kindness was of no earthly use; it was back again at the steps in no time and preferred captivity to freedom.

# Snowbound: A Winter's Journey across the Plains

In the autumn we went into the States and spent most of the winter of 1875–1876 in New York. Colonel Tom and one of the oldest friends we had in the 7th were with us part of the time, and we had many enjoyable hours together. The theater was our unfailing delight. In February we had to say goodbye to all this pleasurable life and return to Dakota, because we had used up all the money we had saved for leave of absence.

When we reached St. Paul the prospect before us was dismal, as the trains were not to begin running until April, at the soonest. The railroad officials, mindful of what the general had done for them in protecting their workers in the building of the road, offered to open the route, sending us through on a special train.

The train on which we finally started was an immense one. There were two snowplows and three enormous engines, freight cars and cattle cars, with stock belonging to the Black Hills miners who filled the passenger coaches. Last of all was the paymaster's car, which my husband and I occupied. At first everything went smoothly. It was intensely cold, but the little stove in the sitting room was kept filled constantly. Sometimes we came to drifts, and the train would stop with a violent jerk, start again, and once more come to a standstill, with such force that the dishes would fall from the table.

One day our speed was checked so suddenly that the little stove fairly danced, and our belongings flew through the car from end to end. Everyone went to inquire as to the ominous stop. Before our train there seemed to be a perfect wall of ice; we had come to a gully which was almost filled with drifts. The cars were all backed down some distance and detached. The snowplows and engines having thus full sweep, all the steam possible was put on, and they began what was called "bucking the drifts." After one tremendous dash, however, the plows and one engine were so deeply embedded that they could not be withdrawn. The employees dug and shoveled until they were exhausted. The Black Hills miners, then the officers and recruits worked until they could do no more.

In this dispiriting and forlorn situation, days passed and seemed to stretch on endlessly. The snow was heaped up about us and falling steadily. All we could see was the trackless waste of white on every side. The wind whistled and moaned around the cars and rocked our frail little refuge from side to side. I made the best effort I could to be brave, but I had no other idea than that we must die there. We tried to be merry, but finally the situation became desperate, and the officers could no longer conceal their concern for our safety.

*The employees dug and shoveled until they were exhausted.*

Search was made throughout the train to find if there was a man who understood anything about telegraphy, for among the fittings stowed away in the car a tiny battery, with a pocket relay, had been found. A man was finally discovered who knew something of operating. The wires of the pocket relay were fastened to either end of the cut main wire outside, making an unbroken circuit between us and our Lincoln friends and uniting us with Fargo station. After that we kept the wires busy, talking with our friends and devising plans for our relief. In a little while the general had an answer from Colonel Tom: "Shall I come out for you?"

Tom went to Bismarck and hired the best stage driver in all the territory to drive to the stranded train.

At last a great whoop and yell, such as was peculiar to the Custers, made me aware that Tom was outside. I scolded him for coming before I thanked him, but he made light of the danger and hurried us to get ready, fearing a coming blizzard. His arms were full of wraps and his pockets crowded with mufflers. We did ourselves up in everything we had. The drifts were too deep to drive near the train cars, so my husband carried me over the snow and deposited me in the sleigh. Then the two brothers followed, and thus packed in, we began that terrible ride, amid the cheers of those we were leaving. It was understood that we were to send back help to those we left.

# THE TELEGRAPH

The telegraph was the first technology ever to use electricity for the purpose of communication. Between 1836 and 1837, the American painter and inventor Samuel F. B. Morse, building on work that had been done in Europe, developed the first telegraph system in the United States. It enabled an operator, using the Morse code system of dots and dashes, to tap out a message with a telegraph key. Relay devices inside telegraph lines then sent the message to its destination. During the 1840s and 1850s, a growing number of lines were installed to connect major American cities, as well as parts of the western prairie. By the time of the Civil War, the Western Union Telegraph Company had extended its service all the way to California, linking the entire country.

The suspense and alarm in the train had been great, but that journey through the drifts was simply terrible. Every time we plunged into what appeared to be a bottomless white abyss, I believed that we were to be buried there. And so we would have been, had it not been for the experience and will shown by the old driver. He had a peculiar yell that he reserved for supreme moments, and that always incited the floundering mules to new efforts. If there had been a tree to guide us, or had it been daytime, it would not have seemed so hopeless a journey. The moon was waning. There was nothing to serve as guideposts except the telegraph poles. The snow never ceased falling, and I knew too much of the Dakota blizzard not to fear that it would settle into that driving, blinding, whirling atmosphere through which no eyes can penetrate.

When at last I saw the light shining out of our door at Fort Lincoln, I could not speak for joy and gratitude at our release from such peril. Our friends gathered about us around the great log fire in the general's room. No light ever seemed so bright as our own fireside. All the help that Bismarck could give was sent out at once to rescue the other passengers, but the train remained in the spot where we had left it until the next spring.

# Our Life's Last Chapter

Our women's hearts fell when the order went forth that there was to be a summer campaign, with probably actual fighting with Indians. Sitting Bull refused to make a treaty with the Government and would not come in to live on a reservation. Besides his constant attacks on the white settlers, driving back even the most adventurous, he was invading and stealing from the land assigned to the peaceable Crows.

The preparations for the expedition were completed, and the morning for the start came only too soon. My husband was to take sister Margaret and me out for the first day's march, so I rode beside him out of camp. The column that followed seemed unending. There were pack mules and ponies and cavalry, artillery, and infantry. The number of men — citizens, employees, Indian scouts, and soldiers — was about twelve hundred. There were nearly seventeen hundred animals in all.

The Indian scouts beat their drums and kept up their peculiar, monotonous tune, which is melancholy beyond description. This they kept up for miles along the road. After we had passed the Indian quarters, we came near Laundress Row. The wives and children of the soldiers lined the road.

Mothers, with streaming eyes, held their little ones out at arm's length for one last look at the departing father.

When our band struck up "The Girl I Left Behind Me," the most despairing hour seemed to have come. All the sad-faced wives of the officers who had forced themselves to smile bravely gave up the struggle at the sound of the music. The first notes made them disappear to fight out alone their trouble.

From the hour of breaking camp, before the sun was up, a mist had enveloped everything. Soon the bright sun began to penetrate this veil and dispel the haze, and a scene of wonder and beauty appeared. The cavalry and infantry, the scouts, pack mules, and artillery, and the long line of white-covered wagons, made a column some two miles in length. As the sun broke through the mist, a mirage appeared, which took up about half of the line of cavalry, and thenceforth for a little distance it marched, equally plain to the sight on the earth and in the sky. The future of the heroic band, whose days were even then numbered, seemed to be revealed, and already there seemed a premonition in the supernatural translation as their forms were reflected from the opaque mist of the early dawn.

The sun, mounting higher and higher as we advanced, took every little bit of burnished steel on the arms and equipments along the line of horsemen and turned them into glittering flashes of radiating light. At every bend of the road, as the column wound its way round and round

*As the sun broke through the mist, a mirage appeared, and for a little distance it marched, equally plain to the sight on the earth and in the sky.*

the low hills, my husband glanced back to admire his men and could not refrain from constantly calling my attention to their grand appearance. There was a unity of movement about them that made the column seem like a broad, dark ribbon stretched smoothly over the plains.

The soldiers, inured to many years of hardship, were the perfection of physical manhood. Their faces, brave and confident, inspired one with a feeling that they were going out aware of the momentous hours awaiting them, but inwardly assured of their capability to meet them. The general could scarcely restrain his joy at being again with his regiment. His buoyant spirits at the prospect of the activity and field life that he so loved made him like a boy. He was hopeful that but a few weeks would elapse before we would be reunited and used this argument to give me courage to meet our separation.

As usual he and I rode a little in advance, and we selected camp that first night on a small river a few miles beyond the post. In the morning the farewell was said, and the paymaster took sister and me back to the post.

With my husband's departure my last happy days in garrison were ended. A premonition of disaster that I had never known before weighed me down, and I could not shake off the influence of depressing thoughts. I shut into my heart the most uncontrollable anxiety. For we heard constantly at the fort of the disaffection of the young Indians of the reservation and of their joining the hostiles.

And we knew, for we had seen for ourselves, how admirably they were equipped.

The first steamer that returned from the Yellowstone River brought letters from my husband, with permission for me to join him by the next boat. I counted the hours until the second steamer was ready. It seemed as if the time would never come for it to depart.

Meanwhile our own post was constantly surrounded by hostiles, and the outer pickets were continually subjected to attacks. It was no unusual sound to hear the drumroll calling out the infantry before dawn to defend the garrison.

A picture of one day of our life in those times is fixed indelibly in my memory. On Sunday afternoon, the 25th of June, our little group of women, borne down with one common anxiety, sought solace in gathering together in our house. We tried to find some slight relief from trouble in the old hymns, some of them dating back to our childhood's days, when our mothers rocked us to sleep to their soothing strains. We all were absorbed in the same thoughts and longings. Yearning for the absent and terror for their safety engrossed each heart.

At that very hour the fears that our minds had portrayed in imagination were realities, and the souls of those we thought upon were ascending to meet their Maker.

On the 5th of July—for it took that time for the news to come—the sun rose on a beautiful world, but with its earliest beams came the first knell of disaster. A

# THE BATTLE OF THE LITTLE BIGHORN

In 1876 President Grant declared war on the Indians who had refused to "come in" to the reservations. He directed Custer's regiment, along with forces commanded by two other generals, to trap the free tribes in the Powder River Country. By late June, Custer was in Montana Territory, hot on the trail of an enormous gathering of Sioux and Cheyenne. On June 25 he tried to attack their camp on the banks of the Little Bighorn River. But he and about 225 of his men were surrounded and overwhelmed instead. Furious warriors led by Crazy Horse, Gall, Two Moon, Lame Deer, and others swirled around the soldiers, swiftly killing them all in a cloud of gunsmoke and dust. The only member of Custer's force left alive on that summer day was a horse named Comanche.

The Battle of the Little Bighorn was the last victory for the Plains Indians. Outraged by Custer's defeat, the army struck back hard. Although the warrior bands had scattered after the fight, soldiers pursued them with a vengeance, even in the dead of the following winter. By spring 1877, the Indians, starving and exhausted, finally gave up. Crazy Horse was killed, and Sitting Bull retreated to Canada, only to return and surrender in 1881. The free life of the Plains Indians was over forever.

steamer came down the river bearing the wounded from the battle of the Little Big Horn, of Sunday, June 25th. This battle wrecked the lives of twenty-six women at Fort Lincoln, and the orphaned children of officers and soldiers joined their cry to that of their bereaved mothers.

From that time the life went out of the hearts of the "women who weep," and God asked them to walk on alone and in the shadow.

*The End*

# Epilogue

Libbie did not actually hear the dreadful news until the morning of July 6, 1876, when officers knocked at the door of her home at Fort Abraham Lincoln. She and Custer's sister Margaret Calhoun, whose husband had also died in the battle, then set out together to inform the other new widows of the Seventh Cavalry.

With remarkable courage, Libbie faced her uncertain future. She moved to New York City, where she lived on little more than her army widow's pension until she began to write.

She was gratified by her literary success, but the Battle of the Little Bighorn had ended the best part of her life. She would spend the rest of it largely in the company of her memories. She surely treasured the last letter she received from her husband, dated June 22, 1876, just three days before he died. It began, "My Darling — I have but a few moments to write, as we move at twelve, and I have my hands full of preparations for the scout. Do not be anxious about me. . . ." It was signed, "Your devoted boy Autie."

# Editor's Note

Elizabeth Bacon Custer was a talented writer who became a professional one during the years of her long widowhood. Her three memoirs describe her life as an army officer's wife, as well as the path of her famous husband's career. *Tenting on the Plains and Following the Guidon* document the period after the Civil War, when General Custer was posted in Texas, Kansas, and Kentucky. *"Boots and Saddles" or Life in Dakota with General Custer,* although the first of her books to be written, tells of the Custers' last years together, from 1873 to 1876.

I have chosen to edit *"Boots and Saddles"* for this series because it offers a "backstage" look at the people and events connected with one of the most dramatic moments in United States history—the Battle of the Little Bighorn. This memoir was emotionally difficult for Libbie to write, but it was also satisfying; it became an immediate best-seller.

*"Boots and Saddles"* is written in a simple, straight-forward style, quite informal for its day and easy to understand. I have, therefore, made only a very small number of changes in the text. Some sentences have been shortened, some spellings have been modernized, and a handful of punctuation marks have been brought

up-to-date. Of course, I have omitted sections of the book for ease of reading. With these exceptions, this is Mrs. Custer's memoir as it appeared when first published, in 1885.

*"Boots and Saddles"* is a primary source, or eyewitness account. I am grateful to have had access to an original 1885 edition of Libbie's work. I have also sought to provide additional background on the struggle between the United States government and the Native Americans for control of the Great Plains. Several of the exciting books I used for my research are listed below. If you are curious to learn more about the frontier days, you might want to read some of these, as well as the books listed in the section "To Learn More about the Custers and the Indian Wars." I hope that you will enjoy them as much as I have.

Brown, Dee. *Bury My Heart at Wounded Knee.* New York: Henry Holt and Company, 1970.

Connell, Evan S. *Son of the Morning Star: Custer and the Little Bighorn.* New York: HarperPerennial, 1984.

*The Custer Reader.* Edited by Paul Andrew Hutton. Lincoln and London: University of Nebraska Press, 1992.

Monaghan, Jay. *Custer: The Life of General George Armstrong Custer.* Lincoln and London: University of Nebraska Press, 1959.

Utley, Robert M. *The Indian Frontier of the American West 1846–1890.* Albuquerque: University of New Mexico Press, 1984.

# Glossary

**agency** the administrative headquarters of an Indian reservation

**ambulance** a wagon usually used to carry wounded soldiers

**annals** written records of events

**artillery** large, heavy guns, such as cannon

**barracks** living quarters for soldiers

**brigadier general** the army rank between colonel and major general

**cavalcade** a procession

**cavalry** soldiers who fight on horseback

**Cheyenne** a tribe of both the southern and northern Great Plains, allies of the Sioux

**citizen** a person not in the military

**command** those soldiers under an officer's authority

**companies** small groups of soldiers within a regiment

**detachment** soldiers ordered to separate from their group to carry out a special assignment

**dispatch** a message

**expostulate** to argue earnestly; to protest

**forage** food for animals

**garrison** a military fort or the troops stationed there

**gauntlets** gloves

**Great Father** an Indian name for the president of the United States

**hostiles** the U.S. government name for Indians who refused to live on reservations

**imperturbable** calm; not disturbed

**infantry** soldiers who fight on foot

**mirage** an optical illusion in which an object appears to be hovering in the air

**mottled** spotted with patches of different color

**plover** a small gray or brown bird that lives near water

**pocket relay** a device used to send a telegraph signal

**premonition** a forewarning; an omen

**Pullman car** a train car with sleeping accommodations

**Ree (Arikara)** a small Plains tribe that often supplied scouts to the army

**regiment** a military unit, such as the Seventh Cavalry

**seminary** an old-fashioned term for school

**sepulcher** a place of burial; a tomb

**Sioux** in the 1800s, the largest and most powerful of the Great Plains tribes

**sirocco** a hot wind

**steamer** a steamship

**sutler** a person who sells food, drink, and other provisions to the army

*travois* a device made of buffalo hide and lodgepole pines used by Indians to move their belongings

**Uncapapa (Hunkpapa)** a division of the Sioux tribe

**verdure** greenery

**veterinary surgeon** a person qualified to care for and to
perform surgery on animals

**vicissitudes** constant changes; the ups and downs of life

# To Learn More about the Custers and the Indian Wars

## Books

Bial, Raymond. *The Sioux*. New York: Benchmark Books, 1999.

Grinnell, George Bird. *When Buffalo Ran*. Washington: Hancock House Publishers, 1993.

Kines, Pat. *A Life Within a Life: The Story and Adventures of Libbie Custer, Wife of General George A. Custer*. New York: Nova Kroshka Books, 1998.

Schomp, Virginia. *Crazy Horse, Heroic Sioux Warrior*. New York: Benchmark Books, 1998.

Taylor, William O. *With Custer on the Little Bighorn*. New York: Viking Penguin, 1996.

## Video

*The West*. New York: PBS Productions, 1996.

## Places to Visit

Custer Battlefield National Monument, Montana

Custer State Park, Black Hills region of South Dakota

The National Museum of the American Indian (A Smithsonian Museum), New York, NY

# Websites*

George Armstrong Custer and Elizabeth Custer
www.generalcuster.net
Information about the Custers, as well as photographs of the site
of the Battle of the Little Bighorn

The Indian Wars
www.cbhma.org
Includes biographies of key figures in the Indian Wars and an
extensive list of related books and videos

The West
www.pbs.org/weta/thewest
An excellent overview of the history of the settling of the West,
based on the PBS series *The West*, directed by Ken Burns and
Stephen Ives

---

* Websites change from time to time. For additional online information,
check with the media specialist at your local library.

# *Index*

Page numbers for illustrations are in **boldface.**

# About the Editor

"Something has always drawn me to the history of the American West. I am fascinated with its dramatic events — the heroic struggle of the Indians to keep their way of life, the extermination of the great herds of buffalo. I also love to read memoirs such as Elizabeth Custer's. Her everyday account ranges from her problems with mosquitoes to the morning she first heard about 'Custer's Last Stand.' It brings the era to life in a very personal way."

In addition to editing Mrs. Custer's work, Nancy Plain has written several biographies and histories. Her biography of the artist Mary Cassatt was a 1995 selection for the New York Public Library's list of *Books for the Teen Age*. Her book *Louis XVI, Marie-Antoinette and the French Revolution*, part of Benchmark's RULERS AND THEIR TIMES series, was named a Notable Social Studies Trade Book for Young People, 2002. The author has three grown daughters and lives in New Jersey with her husband and her dachshund, Molly.